Agincourt

by

Charles Kightly

ALMARK

ALMARK PUBLISHING CO. LTD., LONDON

First published 1974

ISBN 85524 214 0 (paper cover)
ISBN 85524 215 9 (hard cover)

Printed in Great Britain by
Davenport Askew & Co. Ltd.,
24 Wates Way,
Mitcham,
Surrey
for the publishers, Almark Publishing Co. Ltd.,
49 Malden Way, New Malden,
Surrey KT3 EA, England.

CONTENTS

SOURCES

From the French viewpoint, in order of importance:

Chronique de Jehan de Waurin
Chronique de Enguerrand de Monstrelet
Chronique du Religeux de Saint-Denys
Chronique de Ruisseauville
Memoires de Pierre de Fenin
Chronique de Pays-Bas
Chronique des Ducs de Brabant
Chronique de Jean Juvenal des Ursins
Chronique de Gilles de Bouvier, Berry Herald
Chronique de Normandie
Chronique de Tramecourt
Chronique d'Arthus de Richemont
Chronique des Cordeliers
Chroniques de Perceval de Cagny
Journal d'un Bourgeois de Paris
Chronicon Brioceuse

From the English viewpoint, in order to importance:

Gesta Henrici Quinti by Thomas Elmham
Chronique de Jean le Fevre,
Seigneur de Saint Remy
Vita Henrici Quinti
by Tito Livio Forojuliensis
Vita et Gesta Henrici Quinti Anglorum Regis
Historia Anglicana by Thomas Walsyngham
Liber Metricus de Henrici Quinti
Hardyng's Chronicle
Fabyan's Chronicle
English Chronicle 1377-1461
The Great Chronicle of London
Chronicle of Adam of Usk
De Illustribus Henricis
Stow's Annuls
Polychronicon Ranulphi Higden

ABOVE: The Great Helm (which was worn over the bascinet) was used by Henry V in the battle at Agincourt and was later carried in state in the triumphant procession through London.

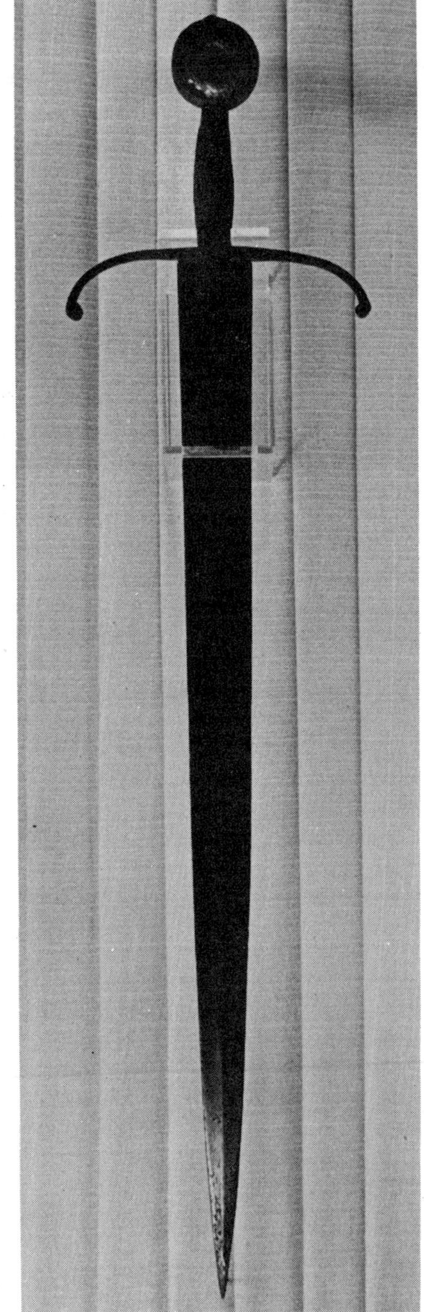

RIGHT: This sword was also used by the King during the battle. It was known as a 'hand-and-a-half' sword. *(By permission of the Dean and Chapter, Westminster Abbey).*

1: The Campaign Begins

The Invasion of France and the Siege of Harfleur

AT THREE o'clock in the afternoon of Sunday, 11th August 1415 King Henry V, just twenty-eight years old and scarcely more than two years on the throne of England, set sail from Southampton in his great ship the *Trinity Royal*, bound for the coast of France. Slipping out of the Hampshire ports and creeks and falling into line behind him came his invasion fleet, no less than 1,500 sail, conveying the English army. On board were about 2,500 knights and men-at-arms with their horses, 8,000 archers, and almost the entire royal household. With them were a vast number of auxiliaries, including priests, surgeons, gunners, armourers, smiths, carpenters, servants and 120 Forest of Dean miners for use in sieges.

At dawn three days later the English army, preceded by its scouts, landed unopposed at Graville (now a suburb of the modern town of le Havre) on the north side of the Seine estuary. It was King Henry's intention to take the nearby port of Harfleur, which controlled the mouth of the Seine, and to hold it as a base for operations against Paris, a hundred miles up-river to the eastward.

The capture of Harfleur, however, was no easy task, for the town was provided with strong walls 2½ miles long, surrounded by a deep moat, and with a garrison who made up for their small numbers with a determination to hold out. For more than a month the defenders made a spirited resistance; all this time they were under constant attack by the English, who not only showered the town with huge stones and flaming projectiles from their great guns and siege engines, but also attempted to undermine its walls. Not until 22nd September, with part of their defences destroyed and their hopes of relief dashed, did the garrison finally surrender.

The English had taken Harfleur, but they were by now in a piteous state. Dysentery, the painful and humilating 'bloody flux', had arisen in the insanitary conditions of a long siege in marshy ground and, exacerbated by the unripe grapes and new wine consumed by the soldiers, had spread throughout the invading army. The Earl of Suffolk and as many as 2,000 others had died of it, and many more were so weakened as to be fit only for immediate repatriation. Thus King Henry's force, even with the addition of some reinforcements recently come from England, was reduced to about 1,300 men-at-arms and 6,000 archers. It was clear, therefore, with his army so depleted, and with winter rapidly approaching, that the King could not carry out his original plan of an attack on Paris, and many of his counsellors urged him to be content with garrisoning Harfleur and returning home.

Henry, however, would have none of this. Partly, no doubt, out of bravado, and partly out of a belief that he could evade or defeat any force the enemy might send against him, he decided to cock a snook at the French, and at the same time enhance his own reputation, by a march through enemy-held territory. The obvious place to head for was Calais, the nearest English stronghold, which was 160 miles to the northward by the shortest route. Henry's confidence of success was increased by the knowledge that the two most powerful local magnates, the Dukes of Burgundy and Brittany, were no more than nominally loyal to the French crown; he may have had secret treaties with one or both of them, and in any case he believed that neither would do much to hinder his march.

Garrisoning Harfleur with 1,200 of his men, King Henry left there all his artillery, most of his auxilliaries, and such of his baggage as could not be carried on pack horses or in a few small carts. Thus lightened, he set off from Harfleur on 8th October with about 6,000 men. They intended to reach Calais in the shortest possible time, and carried rations for no more than eight days.

Despite the King's optimism, many of his commanders believed that the English army would be surrounded and cut to pieces somewhere in the thick woods between Harfleur and Calais. They had good reason for thinking so. The French — despite their weak, mad, King Charles VI, despite the state of near civil war dividing their nation, and despite their failure to relieve Harfleur — were still very much a force to be reckoned with. By the time the English set off for Calais, a French army of at least 60,000 men was concentrating around Rouen and Vernon, not forty miles from Henry's line of march. The English, though they did not know it, were outnumbered by ten to one.

2: The March to Agincourt

FROM HARFLEUR the English army marched northwards, following the coastline. They made good speed, and met with little serious opposition until the 13th October, when they were nearing the river Somme, one of the major obstacles on their road to Calais, which they intended to cross by a ford through the estuary at Blanque-Taque. Shortly before they reached it, however, they received information from a prisoner that the crossing, difficult at the best of times, was guarded by at least 6,000 French troops. This was a disastrous reverse, for unless King Henry retired to Harfleur, which he refused to do, the English had no choice but to turn inland and to march along the south bank of the Somme until a crossing could be found. By now, however, the advance guard of the French army, commanded by Charles d'Albret, Constable of France, and in itself outnumbering the English, was marching along the north bank of the river, shadowing Henry's force and preventing his crossing by breaking down bridges and guarding fords. It looked as if the gloomy prophecies of the King's advisers were being fulfilled.

The 17th October, which according to English hopes ought to have found them safe in Calais, in fact found them at Fouilly, many miles off their route and still unable to cross the Somme. English morale was at a low ebb. Though most of the men-at-arms had horses, some of the archers had walked from Harfleur without a single day's rest. The army's rations were running out, with little hope of replenishment, and many were already existing on nuts and dried meat. The lack of provisions increased the miseries of those suffering from dysentery and fever, and the nights were becoming colder. Nor were the soldiers allowed their traditional solace of plunder, and one of them who stole from a church was promptly strung up from a tree as an example; even more demoralising was the King's order prohibiting the archers from drinking some wine they were lucky enough to find, though wine was apparently allowed to the gentry. On top of all these things, rumours of the huge size of the French army were now rife, and were encouraged by glimpses of large numbers of the enemy on the far side of the river.

It must have been at about this time that the English learnt from prisoners that, when battle was finally joined, the French intended to use knights on armoured horses to ride down their archers. At the suggestion of the Duke of York, therefore, each archer was ordered to cut and carry with him a six-foot stake, sharpened at both ends, which could be stuck into the ground to form a makeshift *chevaux-de-frise*. The usefulness of this invention was to become clear at Agincourt, but at the time that the order was given the bowmen probably only complained of the extra burden.

On the 18th October, when English morale was reaching rock bottom, King Henry received intelligence of two fords over the Somme near Voyennes; both were found to be unguarded, but part of the causeways crossing them had been broken down by the French. Early on the 19th, Sir John Cornwall and Sir Gilbert Umfraville picked their way across with a body of archers and men-at-arms to form a bridgehead. Meanwhile, the causeways were repaired with doors and other fittings from neighbouring houses, and shortly after noon the main body of the English army began to cross the river, encouraged by the King and his officers, who stood on the causeways to prevent panic or congestion. As the first few men reached the north bank, a force of French cavalry appeared, but these were soon driven off by Cornwall's advance guard, and by nightfall the whole English army was across the Somme.

The spirits of Henry's men now rose, and they began to hope that they had given the French the slip. The next day, however, while they were enjoying the first real rest of the march in the village of Monchy-Lagache, King Henry learnt that the enemy had out-manoeuvred him. The Dukes of Orleans and Bourbon, with the entire French army, were a few miles ahead of him at Peronne, and they sent heralds to announce their intention of fighting him before he reached Calais. The English expected a battle almost at once, and accordingly donned their armour and heraldic surcoats. On the following day, however, the 21st October, they were allowed to continue their northward march unimpeded, the only sign of the French being the tracks of thousands upon thousands of horses and men; a sight which deepened the sense of foreboding already felt by Henry's wet and hungry soldiers.

It was not until Thursday the 24th October that the English advance scouts, who had crossed the river Ternoise and mounted a ridge near Blangy, sighted the whole French army, "like an innumerable host of locusts", moving in three vast bodies to cross the English line of march. Henry at once formed up his men on the ridge, and the French, about half-a-mile away on the other side of a small valley, did the same, donning their armour and unfurling their banners.

It may be that some negotiations took place at this time, but if so, neither side found the other's terms acceptable. After a while the French, their myriad lances making them look like a moving forest, began to march away behind Tramecourt wood, intending to block the Calais road. King Henry, suspecting a flank attack or an encircling movement, moved his army to face the direction in which the enemy had gone. With the gathering darkness, however, it became clear from the shouting of grooms and the lighting of fires that the French had camped for the night in and around the villages of Tramecourt and Agincourt. Accordingly, as the pelting rain came on, the English settled down in the orchards and gardens of the hamlet of Maisoncelles to await the morning, and the battle which all of them knew to be inevitable and most of them felt to be hopeless.

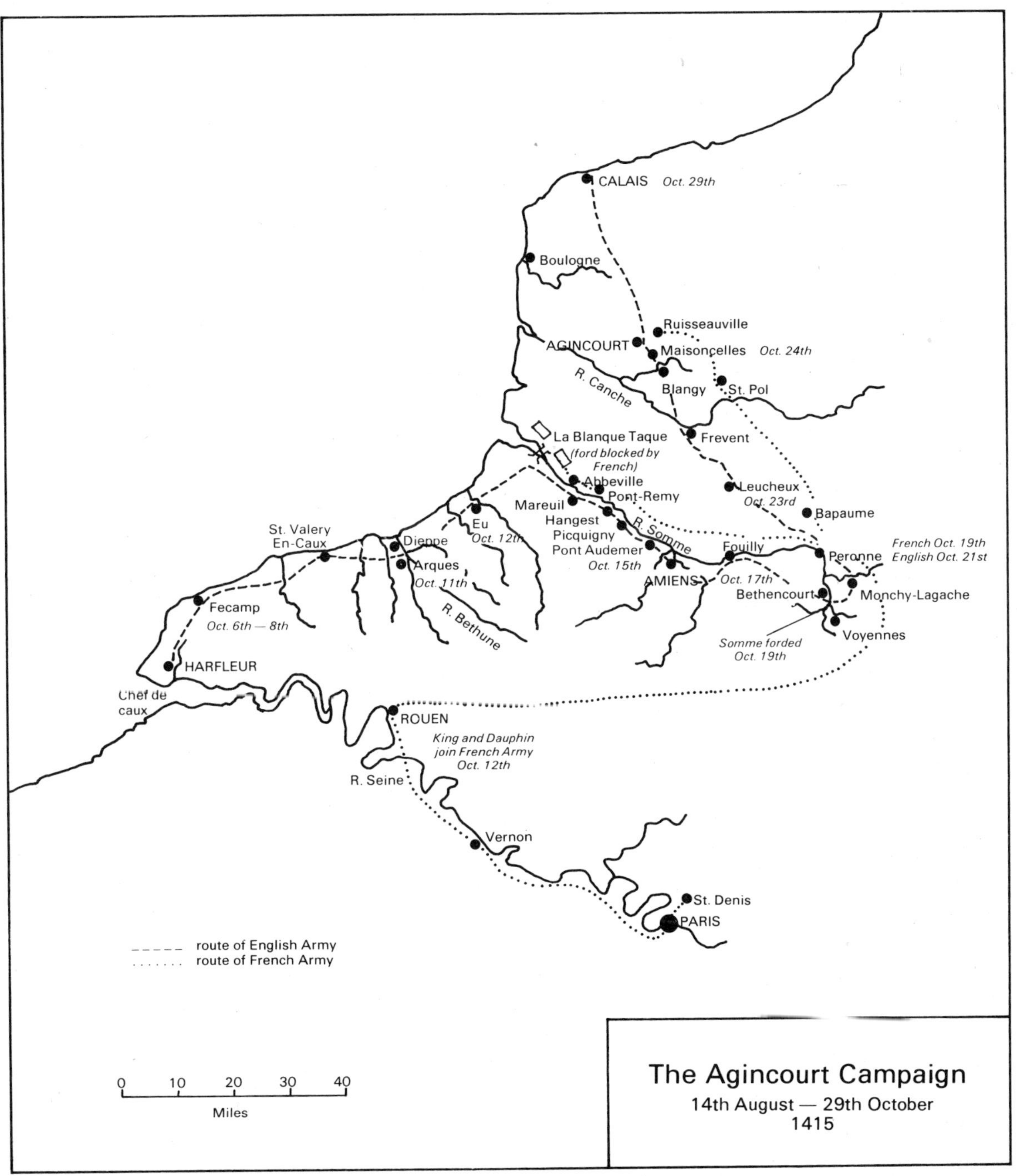

The Agincourt Campaign
14th August — 29th October
1415

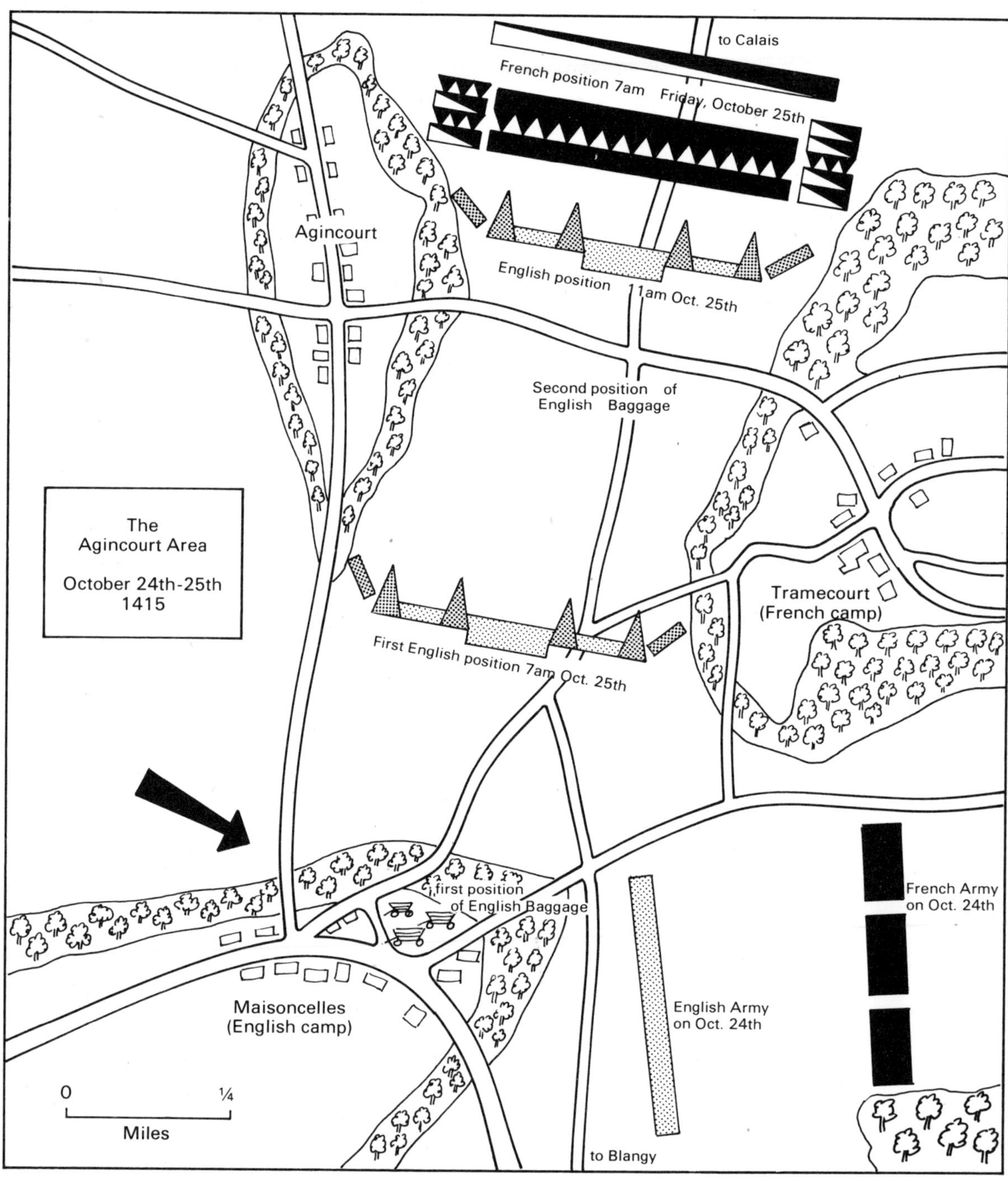

to Calais
French position 7am   Friday, October 25th
English position   11am Oct. 25th
Agincourt
Second position   of
English   Baggage
The
Agincourt Area
October 24th-25th
1415
First English position 7am Oct. 25th
Tramecourt
(French camp)
first position
of English Baggage
French Army
on Oct. 24th
English Army
on Oct. 24th
Maisoncelles
(English camp)
0   ¼
Miles
to Blangy

3: The Night before the Battle

ALL THE chroniclers, both those who were actually present and those who based their accounts on the information of others, stress the contrast between the English and French camps on the night of Thursday 24th August, 1415. The main body of the French, anxious that the English should not now escape, camped more or less where they meant to give battle, athwart the Calais road in the great field between the villages of Agincourt and Tramecourt. This field had been recently ploughed and, being composed of the Picardy mud, notorious to soldiers in the trenches four hundred years later, it was soon reduced to a quagmire by the rain which fell all night, and by the continuous trampling of horses being led up and down by their grooms to prevent them catching cold. Some of the French are reported to have stayed on horseback all night, perhaps to keep their armour clean, but most stood or lay, on straw provided by their servants, round great fires lit near the banners of their principal commanders. Few of them slept, and the English outposts, about a quarter of a mile away, could hear the confused noise of comrade calling to comrade and master to servant. Amidst all the uproar, however, not a horse neighed, and those who noticed this took it for an evil omen. But if the horses were dismayed, the men were supremely confident; it is true that in the last few days they had travelled fast and far, but they were in their own country, they were well fed, and they vastly outnumbered the enemy, whose small numbers and battered condition they despised. Some played dice for the prisoners they were sure of taking in the battle, and others shouted threats to the English sentries, boasting that they would spare none but the King and his nobles, and that all the archers who were taken would have three fingers of their right hands cut off, so that they would never fire a bow again.

Apart from these taunts, there was little contact between the armies during the night. The tale that the Duke of Orleans and the Count of Richemont raided the English camp may be discounted: it appears in only one source, a French chronicler writing many years after the battle, when tales of French heroism were hard to find. Rather more probable is the story that a few English knights were sent out to reconnoitre (as best they could in the darkness) the field where the armies were to clash in the morning.

Though the English advance-guard was within a quarter of a mile of the French, their main body was camped further away, amongst the few houses of the hamlet of Maisoncelles. They found little shelter there from the rain, but some food and drink seems to have been produced and watch-fires were lit. The English had begun the night by making as much noise as their enemies, but the King had soon proclaimed that silence was to be kept on pain of severe punishment: so quiet, indeed, was the camp that some of the French suspected that their enemies had slipped away. There can be little doubt that the prevailing mood in the English army was one of desperation, or, at best, fatalism. All of them, noblemen and archer alike, were exhausted, and many of them still suffered from dysentery, that most debilitating of diseases. For seventeen days they had trudged (on eight days' rations) through a hostile countryside, continually frustrated in their efforts to cross the Somme and continually threatened by a huge, though mostly unseen, French army. They had now seen the enemy, and it was at least as large and well equipped as their fears had made it. For the archers and yeomen who made up five-sixths of the English force there was not even the consolation that their lives might be spared in return for ransom money. It only remained, therefore, to make their peace with God, and those who had not already done so, and who were lucky enough to find one of the relatively few priests, made their confession and took the Sacrament. Others, partly to occupy their minds, mended their armour or re-strung and adjusted their bows. All, said an eye-witness, looked for certain death in the morning.

As the sun rose, at about ten minutes past six on Friday 25th October, 1415, the Feast of Saints Crispin and Crispian, the French and English armies roused themselves from whatever sleep they had managed to get, and began to form up to do battle.

The French Army

Incomparably the larger of the two armies was the French. Nobody now knows how many of them there were, and even at the time no-one seems to have been very sure, since the estimates given by contemporary chroniclers range from 10,000 to 150,000 men. Three eye-witnesses, however, two on the English side and one on the French, all agree that there were between 50,000 and 60,000 men in the French ranks, and this estimate has been accepted here, though it may be rather too high.

As many as three-fifths of the French were men-at-arms — which is to say that they wore armour and fought, either horsed or on foot, with swords, lances, axes and maces. Of these men-at-arms a very large number, perhaps ten thousand, were "gentlemen of coat-armour", ranging from dukes, counts, and barons to obscure knights and poor Picardy squires.

All these gentry wore full suits of armour, the better-off sporting complete suits of steel plate in the latest style, and the lesser men wearing an older style of armour, with a greater mixture of chain-mail. All wore vizored helmets called bascinets, and since their faces could not be seen in battle, they identified themselves by displaying the heraldic arms of their families on a surcoat worn over their armour and, in the case of the greater men, on banners carried before them, round which their retainers rallied.

The remainder of the men-at-arms (perhaps as many as 20,000 of them) were mostly the servants and retainers of the gentry, whose retinues ranged from the hundreds of men whom a nobleman could call on to the two or three family servants brought along by a petty squire. With these retainers were a number of professional soldiers drawn from the garrisons of the castles round Boulogne and also, apparently, some Italian mercenaries from Genoa and Lombardy. It is improbable that all these lesser men-at-arms were fully armoured, but the least well-equipped of them would have worn a steel helmet and a reinforced leather jacket.

Far more poorly equipped, and not to be counted as men-at-arms at all, were the feudal levies of northern and central France, brought to the battlefield by their local "baillis" or royal officials. These peasants, who fought on foot with bow or spear, seem to have been present in considerable numbers, and may have made up as much as a fifth of the French army's total strength.

If the French were comparatively short of anything, it was archers. Despite the fact that within the last sixty years they had three times been decisively beaten by English troops of this type, they seemed unable as yet to grasp the importance of a well-trained and properly used missile arm. It is likely that less than a fifth of their strength were archers, 8,000 of these being longbowmen and 1,500 crossbowmen. Even these, however, outnumbered the whole English army, and could have been used to great effect: but in the event they were brushed aside as low-born, and scarcely employed at all.

If large numbers and high birth were the only factors to be taken into consideration, the French army at Agincourt should have been an invincible force. But as the men-at-arms, up to their ankles in sticky mud, struggled to get into battle array, the flaws in the structures were becoming increasingly obvious. To begin with, the common soldiers were chronically indisciplined, being described by their own side as "bastards, exiles and outcasts, more avid for plunder than accustomed to military discipline, taking no notice of orders." Their indiscipline, however, might have been curbed had the nobles who commanded them been united in purpose—but they were not.

First of all the French nobles were deeply suspicious and jealous of each other; a legacy of years of civil war between the factions of the Orleanists and Burgundians, with each side suspecting the other, not without reason, of selling out to the English. This suspicion did not make for co-operation in the ranks, and nor did the immense and absurd pride which prevented one nobleman from taking orders or even advice from another. Even so the French army might have been made to work together by a single, undoubted leader. In the absence of the mad King and his sons, the French were, in effect, under the direction of a council of war, consisting of the King's nephew, the Duke of Orleans, and other great lords, nominally under the direction of two experienced professional soldiers, Charles d'Albret, Constable, and Jean de Boucicault, Marshal of France.

Neither d'Albret nor Boucicault wanted to bring the English to battle, preferring to pursue the policy of scorched earth and broken bridges which had already been so successful, but they were indignantly overruled by the rest of the council, mostly young men who believed, with all the fervour of ignorance, that one Frenchman, and especially a noble Frenchman, was worth four Englishmen.

The English Army

It is difficult to over-emphasise the differences between the English and the French armies. The French, it will be remembered, numbered about 50,000, three-fifths of whom were men-at-arms, one-fifth peasant levies and one-fifth archers. The English, by contrast, seem unlikely to have mustered more than 6,000 or so, of whom about 1,000 were men-at-arms and the rest archers. The large proportion of archers to men-at-arms was usual in English expeditionary forces at this time, for tactical reasons which will become clear later.

The English men-at-arms were armoured much like their French counterparts, and like them wore heraldic surcoats over their armour. Many of them were also members of the nobility and gentry: apart from the King's brother, Humphrey Duke of Gloucester, and his cousin, Edward Duke of York, the English army contained six earls, sixteen barons, and a large number of knights, esquires and gentlemen. With them fought the clerks, grooms and yeoman of the King's own household, and their ranks were stiffened by professional soldiers of many years' experience —men like Thomas Lord Camoys, Sir John Cornwall and Sir Gilbert Umfraville.

Very different were the 5,000 archers in the English army. Though the French — before the battle — despised them as "people without birth or merit," their countrymen, from the King downwards, recognised that the power of English arms rested on "archers which be no rich men." Upon them had been based the English victories over the French at Crecy (1346) and Poitiers (1356) over the Spanish at Navarette (1367) and over the Scots at Halidon Hill (1332) and Homildon (1402). The bows they carried, made of yew, elm or ash, were five feet or more in length, and needed the same amount of strength to bend them as would be required to lift a sixty-pound weight. When drawn to the ear, these bows were capable of firing a yard long arrow for a distance of 350 yards, though they were accurate only within two-thirds of this distance. Each archer carried with him from two to four dozen arrows, either in quivers or stuck through his belt in sheaves; in action he might, for ease of access, place them in piles at his feet, for the experienced longbowman could shoot at an astonishing speed. In addition to his bow, the archer carried a sword, an axe, or a lead-headed club called a maul, for use in hand-to-hand fighting when his arrows ran out—the English bowman had already shown in several desperate battles that, when required, he could fight manfully alongside the armoured men-at-arms. During the Agincourt campaign, as we have seen, each man also bore a six-foot stake, sharpened at both ends.

Archery was no easily acquired skill, and most of Henry V's bowmen had been recruited in Wales or in the English border counties, however there were also sizeable contingents from Lancashire and Cheshire. Though some of the better-off amongst them may have owned a steel helmet or even a mail shirt, most were simply dressed in a long loose jacket, marked with a red cross of St. George, loose hose, and a protective hat made from boiled leather or wicker strengthened with iron bands. Some did not possess even this rudimentary clothing, and went bare-headed and barefoot. All, after the rigours of the campaign, must have been ragged and filthy.

The English were in some senses a professional army. They were almost all volunteers, raised under a system of contracts called indentures, whereby lords or gentlemen undertook to recruit a certain number of soldiers and the King, in return, guaranteed to pay them and transport them to and from a campaign. The retinues raised in this way ranged from the 142 men-at-arms and 460 archers led by the Duke of Gloucester, through the 17 men-at-arms and 60 archers enlisted by knights like Sir Walter Hungerford, down to the 2 archers who accompanied William Topnell, the King's Master Tailor. Noblemen were paid 6s 8d or more a day, bannerets (the experienced knights who acted as commanders in battle) received 3s, knights got 2s, other men-at-arms 1s, and archers 6d per day. The system of indentures meant that the whole English force, from duke to archer, were paid servants of the King, and this made for greater unity amongst them, helping to reduce the social antagonisms which so bedevilled the French army.

Unlike their enemy, the English were highly disciplined, for the King's articles of war were rigidly enforced. They were not divided politically, and they had one common purpose: to get to Calais, and one undoubted leader: the King. Far from being overconfident, they were desperate men, for the majority of them, the archers, knew that they must either win or die.

4: The Battle

The intended French battle plan

THE FRENCH formed up more or less where they had camped, across the Calais road in the, by now, very muddy fields between Tramecourt on their left and Agincourt on their right, their frontage being reduced to threequarters of a mile by the thickets surrounding the two villages. They marshalled their immense numbers of men-at-arms into three bodies; vanguard, main battle and rearguard, one behind the other: each body was about half-a-mile long and many ranks deep. On each flank of these bodies were posted cavalry on armoured horses. Large numbers of archers and crossbowmen were stationed in front of the vanguard.

The battle, theoretically, was to be begun by these archers, who were to fire volleys of arrows and bolts at the English, while cannon and siege-engines (probably stationed on the flanks of the vanguard) fired great stones at them. Then the armoured cavalry were to ride down the English archers, and afterwards attack the enemy men-at-arms in the flank. Meanwhile the French vanguard and main body, consisting of dismounted men-at-arms, would roll forward and demolish the English main body with one charge, and the rearguard, on horseback, would pursue the fugitives. This was the French plan, and it was, in theory, not a bad one, being probably based on the strategy used at the French victory over the Flemings at Roosbecke in 1382 —a battle in which Charles d'Albret had taken part. Needless to say, not one part of it succeeded.

The plan began to go wrong as soon as d'Albret and Boucicault marshalled the army. Everyone thought that the English would be destroyed in the first charge, so all the great lords wanted the honour of commanding the vanguard, and all those lesser men who could not hope to command it wanted at least to be part of it, if possible in the front line. Everyone pressed forward, until almost the whole van was composed of noblemen and gentlemen, and there were so many banners in it that some of them had to be furled. Even then, it seemed to the watching English that there were more standards in the

French front line than there were lances in the whole English army. In pride of place, in the centre of the front line, was the sacred banner of France, the great red *Oriflamme*, taken from its resting place before the shrine of Saint Denys and carried now by Guillaume Martel.

In the scramble for places in the vanguard, many of the gentry had abandoned their retainers, who retired grumbling and leaderless into the rearguard. Those knights and squires refused a place in the van had got themselves in the main battle of the army, many of them planning to join the forward body as soon as the fighting began. Following his plan d'Albret had sensibly posted 4,000 archers and crossbowmen at the head of the army, but they were now peremptorily ordered out of the way by the nobility in the vanguard, who had no wish to share their victory with such low-born fellows. The archers therefore fell back to the flanks (where they must have got in the way of the cavalry) or placed themselves between the vanguard and the main body.

After much argument, the command of the vanguard, now consisting of about 8,000 dismounted men-at-arms, was divided between d'Albret, Boucicault, and the Dukes of Orleans and Bourbon, assisted by Jacques de Chastillon, Admiral of France, Sir Guichard Dauphin, and the Counts of Eu and Richemont. Thus all the principal commanders of the army — including d'Albret and Boucicault, who should have known better — were risking immediate death in the front line, whereas their proper place was with the main body of the army.

The main body itself, consisting of about twice as many dismounted men-at-arms as the vanguard and stationed fairly close behind it, was commanded by the Dukes of Bar and of Alençon, the last a cautious man previously noted for a prudence which he signally failed to show on this occasion. Amongst the ranks were 12,000 men under the Count of Nevers, younger brother of the Duke of Burgundy, and some of these were knights from Hainault and Brabant (now part of Belgium) who were not subjects of the King of France, but who had simply come along for the fight. It is also likely that the peasants of the feudal levy were placed in the main body.

The rearguard, said by some chroniclers to be the largest of the French divisions, and composed entirely of mounted men, was posted some considerable distance behind the main body, near the village of Ruisseauville. It was commanded by the Counts of Marle, Dammartin and Fauquembergh, but contained very few other gentry, its ranks being filled with leaderless servants and retainers whose masters had found a place in the first two divisions, with professional soldiers from the garrisons round Boulogne, and with a mob of Bretons, Gascons and Poitevins. All these "gros varlets" must have been conscious of the contempt felt for them by the gentry in the vanguard and main body, who meant to defeat the English unaided by their inferiors and to share the glory of victory with no-one.

French Banners

1. The Oriflamme.
   This was the sacred banner of Saint Denis. A few weeks before the battle it was taken from its resting place at his shrine near Paris and delivered to Guillaume Martel, who carried it in the front rank of the vanguard. Martel was killed, but the whereabouts of the banner after the battle are unknown, though there is no record of it being captured.
   The Oriflamme was a gonfanon, which is to say that it hung from a crossbar at right angles to the pole on which it was carried.
2. Banner of the Dukes or Orleans.
   From a contemporary manuscript. The animal is an heraldic hedgehog.
3. The Constable's Standard, about six feet long.

King Henry the Fifth

Born in 1387, he was the son of Henry IV and grandson of John of Gaunt. He fought at the battle of Shrewsbury in 1403 and for several years campaigned successfully in Wales against Owen Glendower and the Welsh rebels. Came to the throne in March 1413. Led the successful Harfleur-Agincourt expedition, August - November 1415. In 1417 he again invaded France and during the next three years conquered Normandy and the surrounding provinces. By the Treaty of Troyes, 1420, it was agreed that he should marry Catharine, daughter of Charles VI of France, and that after Charles' death Henry and his heirs should succeed to the throne of France. He never lived to enjoy that honour, for on 31st August 1422 he died of dysentery contracted at the siege of Meaux. He was succeeded by his infant son, Henry VI.

Henry is shown here wearing his great helm (which can still be seen at Westminster Abbey) encircled by a jewelled coronet. His neck and shoulders are protected by a chain-mail camail covered by a plate bevor. The rest of his body is protected by a complete suit of steel plate armour in the most recent style. It is decorated at the seams with engraved brass. His close fitting surcoat is embroidered with the Royal Arms in heavy gold wire. He wears the insignia of the Order of the Garter below his left knee.

Charles D'Albret, Constable of France

Second cousin of Charles VI of France. An experienced soldier, he had fought the Flemings at Roosbecke in 1382 and against the Moors in North Africa in 1390. Made Constable in 1403, he fought for the Orleanist Party during the civil wars that preceded Agincourt. D'Albret was against fighting a pitched battle at Agincourt, preferring to continue a "scorched earth" policy, but though technically in command, he was overruled by the French nobility. His comparatively sensible battle-plan was ruined by the disorganisation of the French force and he was killed.

D'Albret is shown wearing a complete suit of plate armour. As an extra defence for the neck he wears a heavy hinged bevor. His helmet is a round-topped bascinet with a rounded visor, a style just becoming fashionable in 1415. Over his armour he wears a loose, sleeved surcoat of a type particularly popular in France. The Royal Lilies on his coat of arms reflect his relationship to the French crown. He carries his Constable's Staff of Office and is armed with a sword and ballock dagger.
For D'Albret's banner see page 17

Sir William de Saveuses

Sir William led one of the small parties of French armoured cavalry which attempted to ride down the archers on the English left wing. He was one of the very few to reach the English lines, but his horse stumbled and impaled itself on a stake. He was thrown to the ground where he was finished off by the archers.

Saveuses wears armour like that of D'Albret, but he carries a shield and a lance. His horse's head is protected by an armoured chanfron, its neck by a crinet and its chest and flanks by other pieces of plate armour. Much of the armour is covered by cloth trappers embroidered with Sir William's coat of arms.

Sir Thomas Erpingham

Born 1355. Originally a retainer of John of Gaunt, Erpingham was an experienced soldier, and during the reign of Richard II he had campaigned in Scotland, France, Spain and Prussia. He accompanied Henry IV's invasion of England in 1399 and was made Knight of the Garter in 1400 and Marshal of England in 1404. His retinue for the expedition to Harfleur consisted of five knights, fourteen other men-at-arms, and sixty archers. At Agincourt he marshalled the English army for battle, and had overall command of all the archers. He died in 1428, aged 73.

Sir Thomas is shown wearing a suit of complete plate armour with a pointed bascinet. He wears no surcoat, a fashion just becoming popular at the time of Agincourt, and carries his staff of office as marshal. Round his neck he wears the livery collar of the House of Lancaster, a velvet strip embroidered with the repeated letter S. Such collars were frequently worn by the household officials and retainers of the Lancastrian kings. Below his left knee is buckled the insignia of the Order of the Garter.

For Erpingham's coat of arms see page 28

French Mounted Man-at-Arms

Known as a ''gros varlet'', he might be the retainer of a Lord or Knight or a professional soldier from one of the north French garrisons. Such as he made up the French rearguard and fled the field in thousands after the defeat of the main body.
He wears a steel ''kettle-hat'', a mail camail, and a coat of steel plates to which a cloth covering is attached by metal studs. The latter is marked with the French White Cross of Saint Denis. He wears long leather riding boots rather than leg armour. He is armed with sword and light lance, and rides an unarmoured horse.

Often called a "lance" in contemporary accounts. He might be a professional soldier, a yeoman, or perhaps a member of the minor gentry. He served in the retinue of a Lord or Banneret for one shilling a day. He is completely armoured, but in old-fashioned, perhaps second-hand, armour. His sharply pointed bascinet, snouted vizor, and chain-mail camail are in the style of the 1390's. He wears a plain surcoat embroidered with the Red Cross of Saint George, which all English soldiers were ordered to wear as identification. He is armed with a sword and a pole-axe.

Archers made up five-sixths of the English army and were the main contributors to their victory. He wears a loose coat marked with Saint George's Cross, loose hose turned down for ease of movement and leather shoes. His head is protected by a close-fitting cap made of leather stretched over a wicker frame strengthened with iron bars. He is firing a five-foot longbow tipped with horn at each end. He carried between two and four dozen arrows, some of which he has stuck in the ground in front of him for rapid firing. Protection from cavalry is afforded by the six-foot stake which he was ordered to cut and carry with him.

French Crossbowman

At least fifteen hundred of these served with the French Army, but they were badly positioned and had little chance to use their weapons. This man wears a vizorless bascinet, a camail, and a quilted doublet. He is shown pulling back his bowstring with a mechanical windlass. His crossbow bolts are kept in the painted wood or leather case hanging from his belt.

French Peasant

Thousands of peasant levies, drawn from the northern and central provinces, served with the French Army under their local "baillis" or Governors, many of whom were killed. Armed peasants from Hesdin, Agincourt and the surrounding villages were also amongst those who plundered the English baggage train and threatened the rear of Henry's Army.

This man wears the usual peasant costume of 1415, but is marked as a combatant by the White Cross. He is armed with a short birding bow and a knife.

An English Herald

Taken from a self-portrait of William Bruges, who, as Guienne King of Arms, was present at Agincourt. During the battle the English and French heralds stood together and took no part in the fighting, afterwards identifying the dead by their coats of arms, as shown here. Bruges wears his Herald's tabard over a furred civilian gown.

1

2

3

4

**1 Humphrey
Duke of Gloucester**
Younger brother of Henry V in whose division of the Army he fought. He was wounded in the thigh but rescued by the King and survived to become protector of England after Henry's death. Died 1447.

2 Edward Duke of York
A cousin of Henry's father. Commanded the right wing and was killed, probably by being crushed to death or suffocated.

3 Thomas Lord Camoys
of Trotton, Sussex. A professional soldier, he commanded the left wing.

4 Sir Thomas Erpingham
of Erpingham, Norfolk.

5 Sir John Cornwall
A distinguished soldier, he commanded the bridgehead during the crossing of the Somme. At Agincourt he probably commanded one of the wings of archers, and captured the Count of Vendome.

6 Sir Gilbert Talbot
A Shropshire knight, he had fought successfully against Owen Glendower and the Welsh rebels.

5

6

7

8

7 Richard de Vere,
Earl of Oxford

8 Sir Walter Hungerford
of Farleigh Hungerford, Wiltshire. A royal household official and former speaker of the House of Commons, he fought in the King's division.

9 Sir Richard Kyghley
of Inskip. Commanded a unit of Lancashire archers and was killed.

10 Sir William Phelip
of Dennington, Suffolk. Fought throughout Henry's French wars.

11 Sir Henry Fitzhugh
Lord Chamberlain of England and a diplomat.

12 Roger Vaughan
of Tretower

9

10

Note. In 1415 shields were little used for combat on foot, knights being identified by their coats of arms embroidered on their surcoats or on their banners.

11

12

French Coats-of-Arms

1

2

3

4

5

6

1 Charles Duke of Orleans
One of the leaders of the Vanguard. Captured and remained a prisoner in England until 1440, when ransomed for £33,000.

2 Jean Duke of Bourbon
One of the Commanders of the Vanguard. Had some experience as a soldier and was Captain-General of Guienne. Captured and died a prisoner in 1434.

3 Jean Duke of Alencon
One of the Commanders of the main body but charged in with Vanguard and was killed. Said to have fought very bravely.

4 Antoine Duke of Brabant
Younger brother of the Duke of Burgundy. Arrived late for battle and fought in a make-shift surcoat. Killed during massacre of prisoners.

5 Arthur
Count of Richemont
Brother of the Duke of Brittany. Slightly wounded and taken prisoner. Released a few years later on payment of ransom.

6 John Count of Nevers
Commanded 12,000 Burgundians in the main body. Killed.

7

8

9

10

11

12

7 Robert Count of Marle
One of the Commanders of the Rearguard. Towards the end of battle made a despairing attack with 600 men and was killed.

8 Jean de Boucicault Marshal of France
One of the principal Commanders of the Army, an old soldier who had fought all over Europe and against the Turks. Captured and died a prisoner.

9 David Lord of Rambures
Master of the Crossbows. Killed.

10 Jean Lord of Croy
Killed. Eighteen young knights of his retinue made a pact to attack King Henry and are said to have hacked away part of his crown before they were themselves cut down.

11 Charles Count of Dammartin
One of the Commanders of the Rearguard. Survived the battle and escaped.

12 Sir Clugnet de Brebant
One of the Commanders of the cavalry who attacked the English archers, he avoided their fire and joined in the attack on the English baggage. Over 60 in 1415. Survived and escaped.

1

2

3

4

5

Very differently regarded were the élite cavalry, heavily armoured men on armoured horses, who were posted on the flanks of the vanguard to ride down the English archers. Those on the left — 1,500 of them — were commanded by the Court of Vendome, while the 800 on the right were under an experienced soldier, old Sir Clugnet de Brebant. Both units contained knights famous for their bravery. Also on the flanks were the despised French archers (nominally under the control of the Lord Rambures, master of the crossbows) and the cannons and siege-engines which were to break up the English advance with a hail of stones and cannon-balls. Amongst the artillery pieces, at whose numbers we can only guess, were some "ribaudequins" — an early and highly unreliable form of machine-gun, comprising a large number of small cannon-barrels, which could be fired simultaneously or in series, mounted on a cart. In the event, however, the French artillery did little damage, and even before the battle its field of fire must have been continually obstructed by the press of archers and cavalry.

English Banners

These banners are those stated to have been carried in King Henry's own divisions of the Army. Other lords, and also the experienced Knights called bannerets who acted as Battalion Commanders, will have carried banners of their own coats of arms. Banners were usually about four feet square.
1. The Royal Arms of England
2. The Cross of Saint George
3. The Arms of Saint Edward the Confessor. These arms were also used by both Richard II and Henry V.
4. The Banner of the Holy Trinity, to which Henry had a special devotion.
5. Lancastrian Family Insignia.
   The foxtail hanging from a pole painted in the blue and white colours of the Lancaster family was also used by Henry IV and by Henry VI.

The French army must have been formed up by seven o'clock, but far from moving to the advance, as the English expected, the massive divisions remained stationary. Banners were stuck into the ground and men stood or sat in companies around them, eating what breakfasts they had, making up old quarrels, and some of them shortening their fourteen-foot lances to a more manageable length for combat on foot. It is apparent that the hotheads in the French council of war had been overruled by d'Albret and the old soldiers, who wisely reasoned that it would be disadvantageous to attack, through thick mud, an enemy with a comparatively powerful missile arm. With the French blocking the road to Calais the English, vastly outnumbered, must either surrender, starve to death, or attack at a disadvantage.

The English form up

King Henry, who had been sleeping in one of the few houses in the hamlet of Maisoncelles, rose before dawn, and at once his esquires and pages helped him into his armour, a complete suit of steel plate covering him from chin to toe. For the time being he left off his helmet, but donned a surcoat embroidered with the lions of England and lilies of France. Priests then came to him, and he devoutly heard three masses, one after the other. Meanwhile, throughout the hamlet and the surrounding area, cold, wet, men were emerging from barns, byres and hedge-bottoms, half-expecting, perhaps, that the French would fall on them immediately. Those who had any food left ate it, and everyone, checking their weapons and armour, formed up in companies round the banners of the lords and captains.

As soon as the King's last mass was finished, he put on his helmet, over which was a gold crown decorated with precious stones and, without sounding any trumpets, he quietly gave orders for the English to move out of Maisoncelles, and to form up in a field

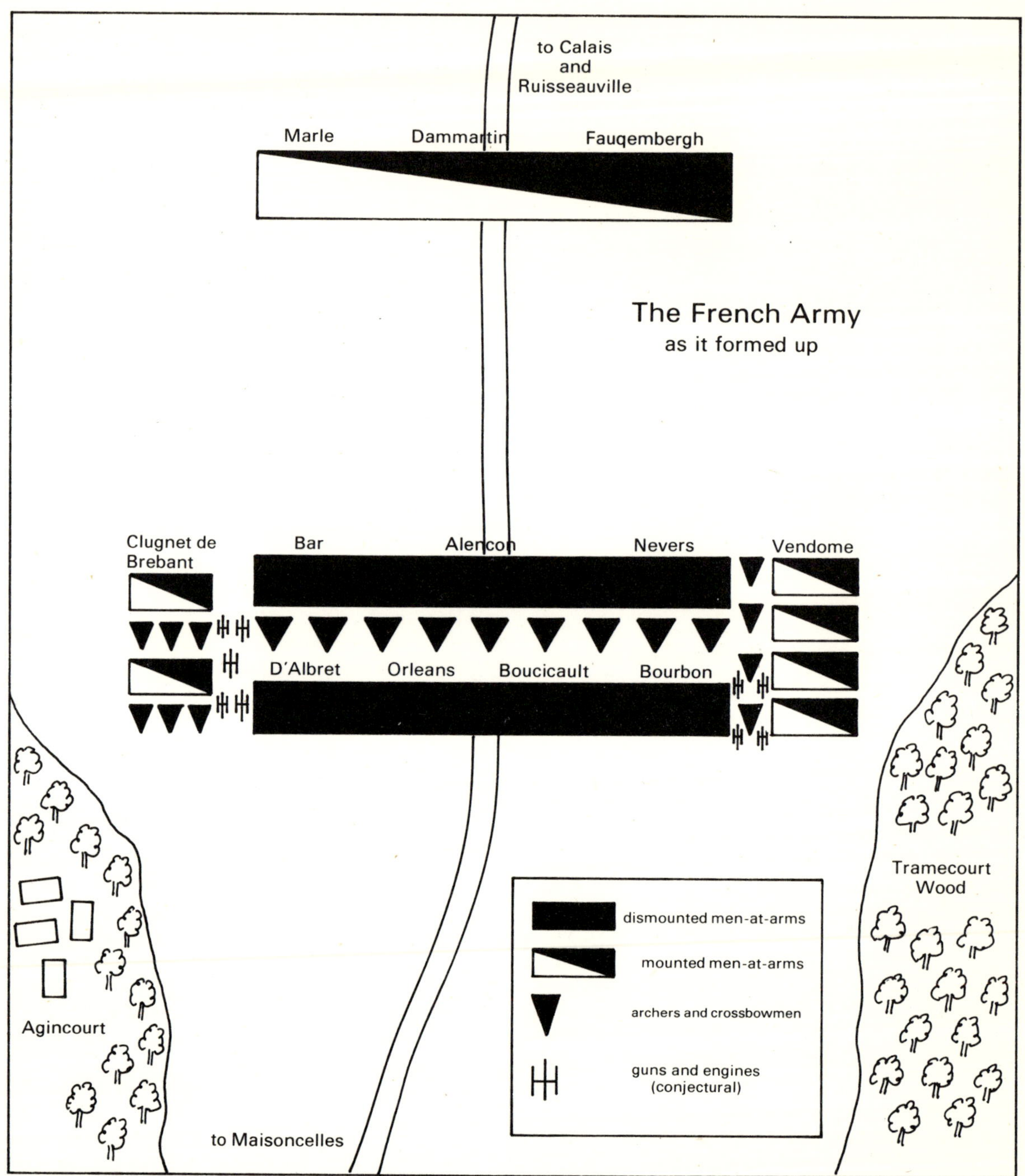

to Calais
and
Ruisseauville
Marle
Dammartin
Fauqembergh
The French Army
as it formed up
Clugnet de
Brebant
Bar
Alencon
Nevers
Vendome
D'Albret
Orleans
Boucicault
Bourbon
Agincourt
to Maisoncelles
Tramecourt
Wood
dismounted men-at-arms
mounted men-at-arms
archers and crossbowmen
guns and engines
(conjectural)

of newly-planted corn, facing the enemy who could be seen forming up about a thousand yards away. The baggage train, including part of the crown jewels, all the spare horses, the acutely sick, and the pages who were too young to fight, was for the time being left in Maisoncelles, in the care of ten men-at-arms and twenty archers; a meagre protection, but all that could be spared.

King Henry expected to be attacked, and the position which he began to take up by 6am was essentially a defensive one. The woods and hedges surrounding Agincourt and Tramecourt, which restricted the French frontage, served to protect the flanks of the far smaller English force, while the hamlet of Maisoncelles, with its orchards and buildings, would help to break the impetus of an enemy charge from the rear. It only remained, then, to fill as much of the space between Agincourt and Tramecourt woods as possible: to do this, Henry would have to marshal his forces in one long line, not allowing himself any reserves.

The English men-at-arms, all on foot, were divided into three bodies each containing about three hundred men, drawn up in ranks four deep. In the centre of the line was the body commanded by the King himself, and marked by his five banners — the arms of England and France, the red cross of St. George, the blue and gold flag of St. Edward, the red and silver banner of the Trinity, and the badge of the house of Lancaster, a fox-tail tied to a blue and white pole. To the right was the vanguard, commanded at his own request by the Duke of York, and to the left was the rearguard under Thomas Lord Camoys, a Sussex man with military experience going back more than thirty years. In the spaces between the bodies of men-at-arms were the archers, formed up in wedge-shaped formations protruding forwards from the line so that they could fire not only into the faces, but also into the sides of the approaching enemy. The French would also have to suffer the frontal and flanking fire of large bodies of archers drawn up on the extreme outer edges of the English army.

As the English army formed up, the men-at-arms clustering round the banners of their leaders, and the archers driving in their pointed stakes to protect themselves from cavalry, the King rode up and down the line on a small grey horse, his great white charger and his other horses, splendidly caparisoned, being led along behind him by his household. He had already promised that he would never allow himself to be captured, and now he rode without spurs, to show that if his army were defeated he would not ride away from them. From time to time he stopped and spoke to groups of as many men as could hear him.

He told them that he had entered France to recover his lawful inheritance, and that his claim to the French crown was a just one; that they should remember that they were born in England, where their parents, wives and children dwelt, and to which therefore they should strive to return with fame and glory; that their ancestors had gained many victories over the French, and that every man there should fight for his own honour and for that of the English crown. Most important of all, he reminded them of the French boast that they would cut three fingers from the right hand of every English archer. Everywhere the King was cheered by his army with cries of "Sire, God give you a good life, and the victory over your enemies".

The waiting

All this time, every English eye not fixed on the King was focussed on the French army, which could be clearly seen, a thousand yards away across the flat fields. Everyone expected the vast glittering mass, flanked on either side with cavalry, to bear down on them at any moment, but fairly soon it became clear that the French had no intention of moving. For fully three hours, between seven o'clock when the armies must both have been fully drawn up, until after ten, the English and the French stood staring at each other. What

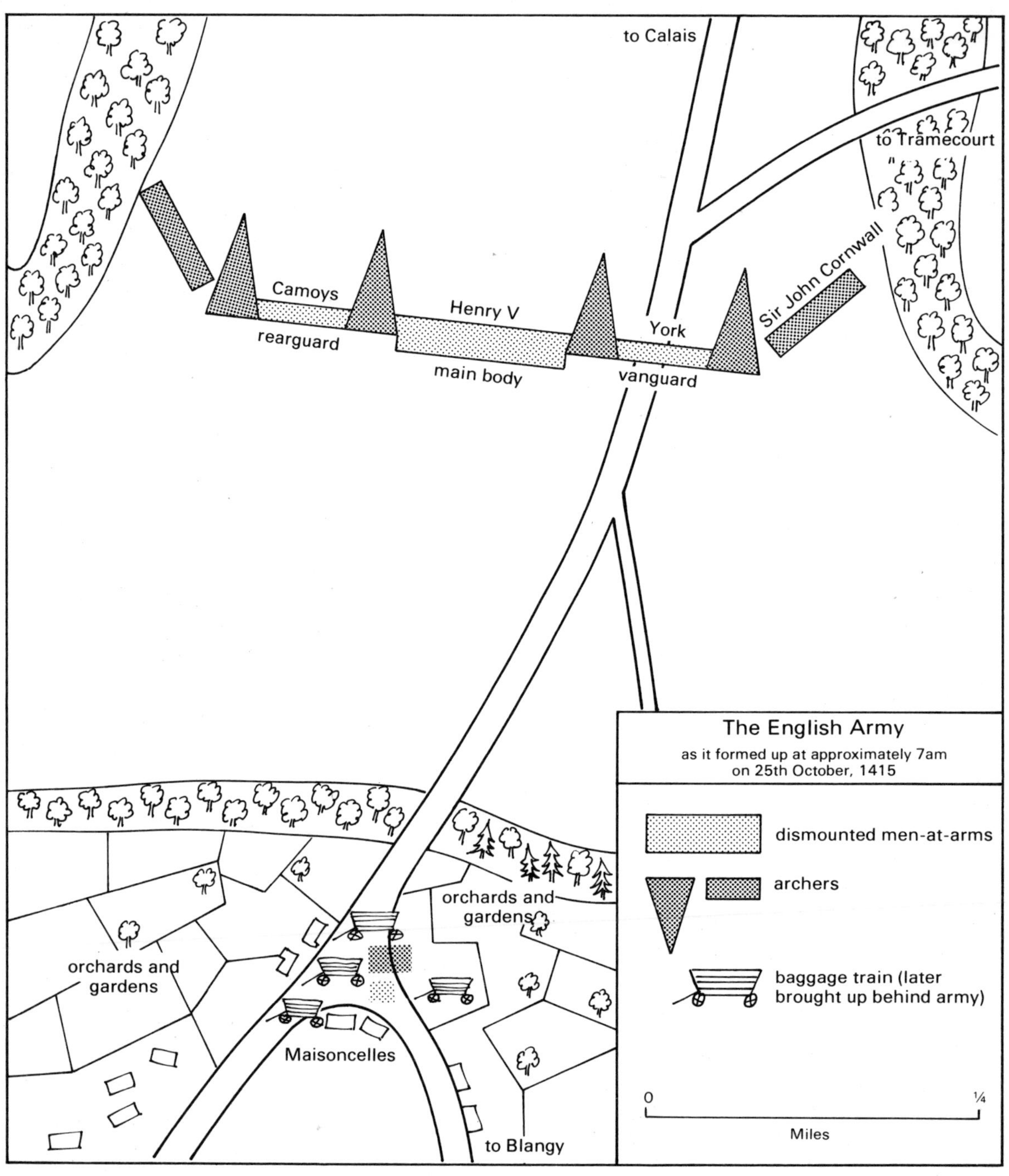

to Calais
to Tramecourt
Camoys
rearguard
Henry V
main body
York
vanguard
Sir John Cornwall
The English Army
as it formed up at approximately 7am
on 25th October, 1415
dismounted men-at-arms
archers
baggage train (later
brought up behind army)
orchards and
gardens
orchards and
gardens
Maisoncelles
to Blangy
0
¼
Miles

actually happened during this time is a matter for dispute, even amongst eye-witnesses. The French believed that King Henry ordered 200 archers to move forward under cover of the Tramecourt woods, ready to fire into the flanks of their vanguard as soon as battle was joined, but an eye-witness on the English side categorically denies the story. They also believed that a party of English skirmishers somehow got into Agincourt, behind the French lines, and set fire to a barn there. This arson, however, is more likely to have been effected by local scavengers out for plunder. The same peasants could be seen hanging about Maisoncelles, hungrily eyeing the English baggage there.

What is certain is that the three hours or more of waiting, intolerable for any man expecting death, was worse for the English than for the French, and many of King Henry's men must have realised that, with every minute that passed, the situation was becoming more and more desperate. They had little or no food, and no prospect of getting any; they could not retire, and yet the enemy blocked their route home; and the French army, already vastly outnumbering them, was being reinforced hourly, whereas their own numbers could only decrease. It is even said that the King himself, despairing, sent emissaries to the French, offering to give up his claim to the French throne, and the town of Harfleur, in return for a safe passage to Calais and certain other guarantees. If these negotiations ever took place, however, they came to nothing.

What finally seems to have goaded Henry into a decision was the arrival from the French army of the Sieur de Heilly and two other knights, ostensibly on business connected with Heilly's personal honour but more probably to spy on the English dispositions. The King asked Heilly to take a message to the French commanders, desiring them to begin the action, and when the knight rudely refused to do so, Henry rounded on him saying; "Go back to your army, but however fast you go, we shall not be far behind you." Against all the rules of warfare, the little English army was committed to attacking an enemy ten times its size.

As the position they had already taken up demonstrated, however, the English commanders knew very well that their army was more effective in defence than in attack, and that their only real chance of victory lay in drawing the enemy onto the fire of their archers. It was therefore decided that the English would march forward in formation until they were within bowshot of the French, and then halt and take up a new defensive position, hoping by some means to lure the enemy into attacking them.

Now, at last, the order to advance was given, the King shouting out: "In the name of Almighty God and Saint George, advance banners, and Saint George this day be thy help." Before moving forward, however, each man in the army knelt three times, making the sign of the cross on the ground and then kissing it, taking as they did so a small piece of earth into their mouths. By this pious ceremony they imitated the Holy Communion and acknowledged that they were mortal — but at the same time they indicated that they were prepared to die where they stood rather than flee. Then rising to their feet, they gave three shouts which, says an eye-witness, greatly amazed the French, and advanced over the muddy fields, with a great noise of trumpets, clarions, horns, pipes and drums. The men-at-arms moved forward in echelon — first the vanguard, on the right, then the main body, and then, on the left, the rearguard — with the archers keeping station and carrying their sharp-pointed stakes. Once or twice they stopped to allow the armoured men to draw breath, and each time they moved on again they gave another loud cry. When they were within bowshot (about 200 yards) of the French, the whole army halted. The archers drove their stakes into the soft ground, and immediately began to shower the enemy with arrows.

The French Cavalry Attack

At first, it seems, the English advance took the French completely by surprise. None of them really expected Henry and his battered followers to do anything but surrender, and it is quite clear that the French commanders were unprepared for action, with their army not properly marshalled. At the sound of the first English shout, knights who had been visiting their friends in other parts of the army, or seeing to the feeding of their horses at the rear, made frantic attempts to resume their proper places in the line. The rest put on their helmets, said their prayers, and embraced each other, while the Constable d'Albret and the other French generals exhorted them to fight bravely.

The disorder which already existed in the French ranks turned to something like chaos when the English archers fired their first vollets, their arrows descending as thick as hailstones. Men were already beginning to fall everywhere, and the men-at-arms hunched themselves forward as if in a rainstorm, so that the arrows would not pierce the slits in their vizors. On the crowded flanks, hemmed in between the woods on one side and the massed vanguard on the other, some of the French archers and crossbowmen succeeded in loosing off a few hasty and ill-aimed shots at their tormentors. Being unarmoured, however, they were soon forced to retire by the far more rapid and accurate English fire. A few of the French guns, too, managed to fire, and at least one English bowman, named Roger Hunt, is known to have been killed by a cannon ball.

The French battle plan, it will be remembered, provided for squadrons of heavily armoured cavalry to be stationed on both wings of their army, in order to ride down the English archers. These were now ordered forward, but of the 2,000 men assigned to the task, only about 400 could be found in the confusion. No charge is known to have been

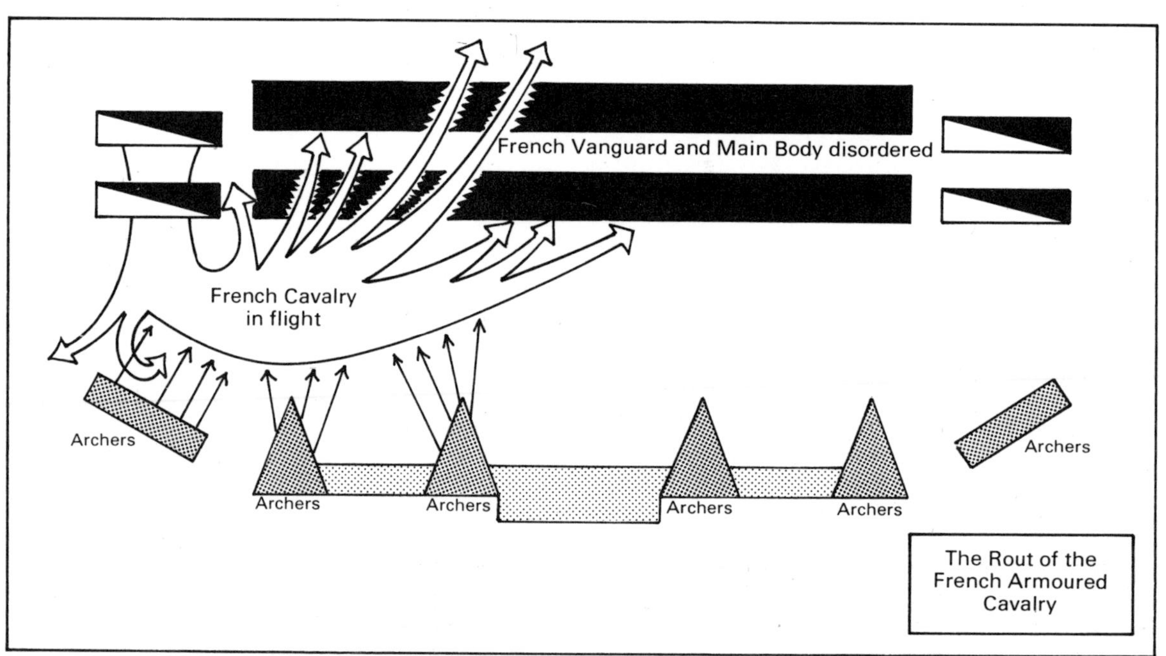

attempted on the Tramecourt side of the field, but on the Agincourt side 300 men rode out under Sir William de Saveuses, "a very brave knight."

Saveuses' task was hopeless from the first: hemmed in on his right by the woods, he and his men could not outflank the enemy, but were forced to come at them head on, riding straight into a cloud of arrows fired at close range. To make matters worse, the horses, not only loaded with the weight of an armoured man but partially armoured themselves, were slowed down to stumbling pace by the thick mud. The closer they got to the English line of stakes, the thicker came the arrows. Wounded horses reared and plunged, throwing their riders and then falling on top of them; knights, with arrows piercing the joints in their armour, fell dead from their mounts. Men said afterwards that the English "shot never arrow amiss," and that they aimed like men shooting for a wager — the wager, in fact, of their own lives.

It was too much for the French. Saveuses and a handful of others charged home, but their stumbling horses were impaled on the pointed stakes, and they themselves were thrown to the ground, where the archers prised open their armour and stabbed them with long knives, or battered them to death with clubs. Others, under Sir Clugnet de Brebant, rode into the woods and thickets to avoid the English fire, and eventually emerged near King Henry's baggage train, which they began to plunder. The majority of the French cavalry, however, turned tail and fled, or were carried to the rear by their wounded horses.

Soon little knots of mounted fugitives, inter-mixed with riderless horses, were crashing into the front rank of the dismounted French vanguard, which was just beginning to advance. The sheer weight of the armoured horses ploughed great gaps through the closely-packed footmen. Men-at-arms were knocked down and ridden over left and right, and to add to the physical damage they did, the fleeing riders spread despondency and alarm wherever they went; many left the field at once, taking with them parties of faint-hearts from the rearguard. So great, in fact, was the chaos caused by the broken French cavalry, that some afterwards believed the panic to have been due to an English mounted ambush emerging from the woods.

The Infantry Battle

The archers had defeated the French cavalry, but the English were still in terrible danger, for now the enemy vanguard — equal in size to the whole of Henry's force — was bearing down on them. As they came, they shouted out their war-cries "Monjoie Saint Denis," "Dieu aide au premier chrêtien," "Malo au riche duc," "Au feu," and in reply the English blew their trumpets and cried out "Saint George, Saint George for Guienne."

At first the French advanced in line abreast, plodding heavily through the thick mud, their heads down and their shoulders hunched against the arrows which the archers were firing at them as fast as they could bend their bows. Soon, however, the line broke up into three columns, as those who found themselves opposite groups of archers veered away and made for the three bodies of English men-at-arms. Then, as the younger or lighter-armed men, anxious for glory, outstripped their comrades, the columns formed themselves into tightly-packed wedges, whose points were aimed at one of the three groups of banners marking the position of the Duke of York on the right, the King in the centre, and Lord Camoys on the left.

With a deafening crash of metal on metal, the three wedges struck the English line, and by their sheer weight sent it reeling backwards some twelve feet. At the same time two bodies of French knights, under the Count of Vendome and Sir Guichard Dauphin, attacked the archers on the wings. The English priests, watching from amongst the baggage train, saw defeat looming, and fell on their knees to beg God to save their countrymen from death.

If the French could now have pressed home their attack, the English army must have broken. But the tightly-packed slow-moving columns, bogged down in the mud as they were, could not maintain their momentum, and very soon they were in difficulties themselves. The archers on the wings, having easily driven off the attacks made on them, poured arrows into the flanks of the French formations, while the English men-at-arms re-formed and counter-charged, driving back the heads of the enemy columns and regaining the ground that had been lost.

The French vanguard was now in a state of chaos: the columns were so tightly packed that only the first two ranks could use their weapons, while the twenty or more ranks behind them could not so much as raise their arms for the press of their comrades. As the English men-at-arms, hacking, slashing and thrusting, killed men in the enemy front ranks, so those behind were inexorably pushed forward. Many fell over the dead bodies and were suffocated as others fell on top of them. Those who fell wounded by arrows, or who fainted in the crush, were trampled to death: more Frenchmen, in fact, were suffocated or crushed to death by their own countrymen than died at the hands of the English.

Many of the archers, seeing the confusion the French were in, now dropped their bows and, drawing their swords and axes from their belts, or picking up discarded weapons from the field, gleefully charged into the fight. The French men-at-arms, crushed together as they were, and able to see only through narrow slits on their vizors, were almost powerless against this new wave of agile, highly-armed opponents. Even if the armoured men could free their arms to deliver a ponderous blow, the bowmen could frequently dodge it. Wherever they could see a gap in the enemy ranks, the archers forced a way in, crushing helmets and skulls with blows from their leaden mauls and stabbing at weak points in French armour with their long knives. Meanwhile, some of their com-

rades still kept up a withering fire into the ranks of the French main body, which was still moving forward to the attack.

Hard fighting was now general all along the line of battle, but it was fiercest around the three groups of English banners, where the French, now harrassed in the flanks and rear by the archers, were still battering away at the men-at-arms. The English right wing was particularly hard hit and its commander the Duke of York, a fat, heavy man, was knocked down and crushed, or smothered, to death: nearby the young Earl of Suffolk was killed. On the left wing Lord Camoys was hotly engaged, at least one of his esquires being cut down as he fought near his master.

Fiercest of all, however, was the fighting round the King's own banners, in the centre of the English line. King Henry's valour that day, said a witness, would have won him glory even if he had been a common soldier and, while this statement may perhaps be dismissed as a sycophantic exaggeration, it is clear that the King was in the greatest possible danger. His banners marked his whereabouts, and must have acted as a magnet for any Frenchman seeking honour and fame. Many of Henry's guards — including three Welsh esquires, his old comrades-in-arms of the wars against Owen Glendower — were cut down around him, and at one time his brother Humphrey was wounded in the thigh and fell half-dead to the ground. Henry stood over the body, beating off the French until Gloucester could be carried to the rear. It was perhaps at this time that he was attacked by a band of 18 young men from the retinue of the Sieur de Croy, who before the battle had sworn to hack the crown from Henry's head or die in the attempt. They did both: one of them, it is said, struck the King such a blow with an axe that he knocked him to his knees, and cut one of the *fleurs-de-lis* from his crown. At once Henry's guards closed round his assailant. and he and his companions were hacked to pieces. To corroborate the story, a great dent can still be

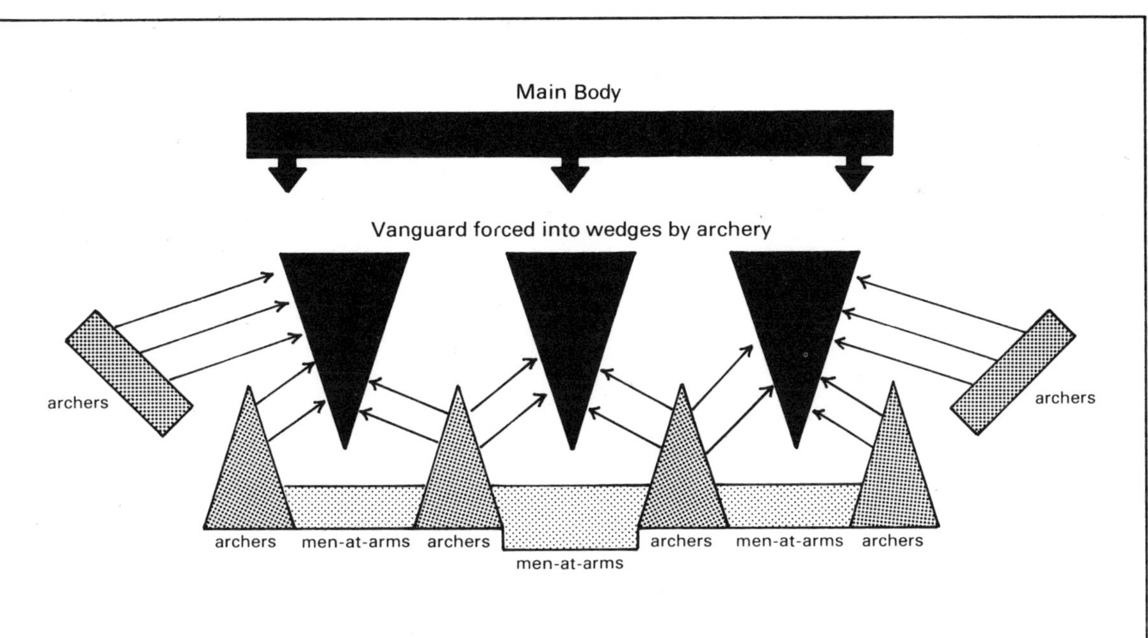

The Defeat of the French Columns

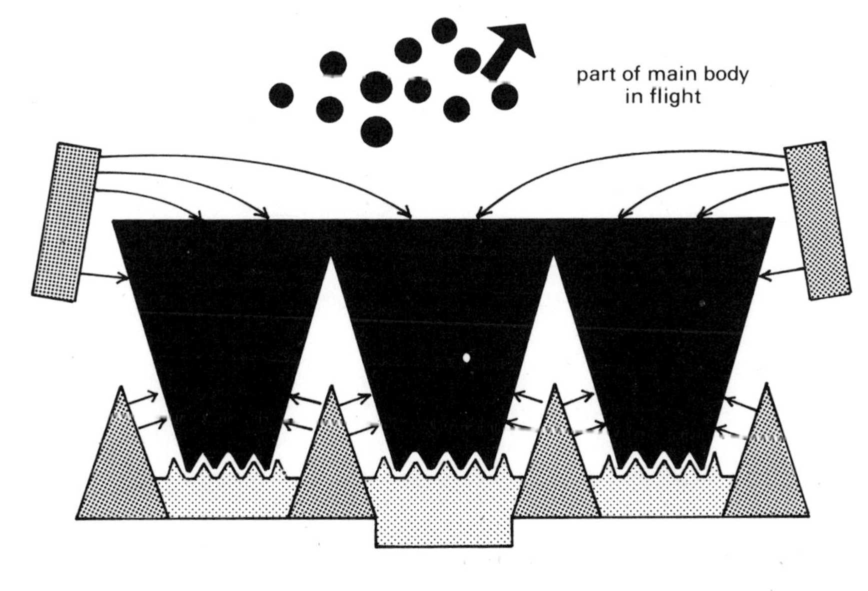

seen in Henry's helmet, which hangs today over his tomb in Westminster Abbey.

Before very long the heaps of bodies — the dead mingled with the living who were pinned down and unable to rise — were piled six feet high in front of the three groups of English banners, and Henry's men had to climb over them in order to hack at the Frenchmen who still pressed forward. The King's battalion was the first to destroy the column of the enemy vanguard that opposed it, and Henry was about to go to the aid of his right wing, still heavily engaged, when he saw part of the French main body bearing down on him and advanced to meet it.

Even now, with their vanguard destroyed after two hours of hand-to-hand fighting, the French thirst for glory was unassuaged. The Duke of Alencon, for instance, who was normally a prudent man, and who had been given command of part of the French main body, left his command and went charging in after the vanguard, only to fall by the hand of some anonymous soldier.

Still more gallant, and more foolish, was the young and much-beloved Duke of Brabant, brother of the Duke of Burgundy. When news of the impending battle reached him, the Duke had been far away in Louvain, in what is now Belgium. By riding day and night, and outstripping all but the swiftest of his followers, he reached Agincourt some time after the battle had begun, but found that his armour and surcoat had been left behind in the rush. Refusing to wait until they arrived, he borrowed his chamberlain's armour, and, cutting a hole in a trumpet banner, he thrust it over his head as a surcoat and rushed into the fight shouting "Brabant, Brabant." He crashed into the English line just behind the wreck of the French vanguard, and in a few minutes his retinue had been cut down and he himself had been taken.

Following his example, parts of the French main body continued to move towards the battered English. Now, at last, Henry's men-at-arms moved forward, and, marching round the piles of bodies in front of their long-held positions, they advanced on the French, accompanied by bodies of archers. Shaken and amazed by the fate of their vanguard, the remnants of the French main body put up little resistance. Those who stood their ground were killed or taken, but most fled towards the rear, where the Counts of Marle and Fauquembergh were desperately trying to rally the rearguard.

The French rearguard, all mounted, was perhaps half as big again as the whole English army, and if it had delivered one really determined charge at this moment it might well have completely broken Henry's battered force, exhausted as it was by desperate fighting. Such a charge might perhaps have been made, had it not been for the rigid social divisions within the French army and the unthinking pride of the French nobility. For the rearguard, it must be remembered, was composed of servants, retainers and mercenaries, who had been considered unfit company for the gentlemen in the first two divisions. Now, bereft of their usual leaders and seeing the nobility dead or in flight, many of the rearguard also began to leave the field. They had, after all, been treated as men without honour; now they were acting as such.

The English were too exhausted to pursue the fugitives. For a few moments the men-at-arms and archers stopped and looked about them, suddenly conscious that the deafening clash of weapons on armour had ceased, and scarcely able to believe that the French had, at least temporarily, been driven off.

The Massacre of the Prisoners

The English did not long remain inactive. Freed for the time being from the necessity of defending themselves, their thoughts turned to the French prisoners, whose ransoms could make some of them rich for life. Few prisoners had been taken during the first crisis of the fight (one French noble had tried to surrender ten times before finally being cut down) but as the enemy formations had been broken up, more and more captives had been secured. With their weapons taken away and their helmets removed, these were now interrogated as to their name and rank, and the most important were taken to the King, who, as one witness observed, seemed to be very cheerful. Excited speculation and argument broke out over the possible value of the rest of the prisoners.

Meanwhile, the archers were pulling down the piles of bodies, separating the dead from the living and seizing upon anyone who could be identified by his heraldic surcoat as a nobleman or a knight. In this way they found the Dukes of Orleans and Bourbon, the Count of Richemont, the Marshal Boucicault and many others, all unhurt or only slightly wounded. The prisoners stood about in forlorn groups, bitterly ashamed of having fallen into the hands of the despised and low-born archers. Soon, it is said, the captives were so many that they outnumbered the whole English army.

In the midst of all this activity, the situation once again changed suddenly and dramatically. Messengers rushed to the King with the news that the French were plundering the baggage train and threatening the rear of the army. As soon as the battle had started, a local squire called Ysambart d'Azincourt, with a rabble of peasants, had fallen on part of the baggage that had been left behind in Maisoncelles. During the crisis of the battle, when the few baggage-guards had left their posts to join in the fight, the plunderers had carried off many of the English horses, and also part of Henry's royal regalia, including a crown, a state sword, gold plate, jewels, and part of the True Cross. Now, joined by some of the fugitive cavalry who had charged on the flanks, and by thousands of scavengers from Hesdin and the surrounding area, the plunderers showed signs of moving against the rear of the English army.

Far worse than the news from the rear, however, was the fact that a body of enemy cavalry and infantry, at least as large as the whole English army, could now be seen forming up in good order as if for a new frontal attack. This force was in fact made up of the remnants of the rearguard, who had with great difficulty been rallied by the Counts of Marle and Fauquembergh, together with some of the fugitives from the main body who hoped to retrieve their lost honour.

The English were now in a situation which was potentially worse than ever. Exhausted as they were, with many of their weapons broken and useless, they were faced with a large body of fresh enemy troops to their front, while another force of unknown size threatened their rear. In their very midst were thousands of prisoners, unharmed and partly armoured, who when battle was rejoined would undoubtedly snatch up weapons and set upon their captors.

From the English point of view, there was only one thing to be done. The King had his trumpets sounded, and ordered that all the prisoners, except those of very high rank who were in his own custody, should at once be put to death. At first many of the English refused to kill their captives — not, it must be added, out of a sense of humanity, but out of disgust at losing the ransoms they would bring. Henry had to threaten to hang anyone who did not carry out his orders, and to make doubly sure he sent out a squire and 200 archers to begin the grisly work. The bareheaded prisoners were decapitated, or had their skulls crushed and their throats cut. More horrible still, the huts into which some of the French wounded had been taken were set on fire, and the helpless men within were burnt to death. Amongst those killed was the Duke of Brabant, whose makeshift surcoat went unrecognised.

This is no place to discuss the morality of the massacre; suffice it to say that the contemporary chroniclers regarded it as an unfortunate necessity. The English bemoaned the loss of the ransom money, while French witnesses attributed the blame for the killings, not to the English, but to the "cursed assembly of men" who threatened to renew a battle which their betters had given up for lost.

With the threat from the prisoners neutralised, the English now turned to face the body of Frenchman moving to attack their front. Once again the archers fired their volleys of arrows, and those of the enemy who were mounted turned and fled. The Counts of Marle and Fauquembergh, however, led some six hundred dismounted men-at-arms in a last despairing charge, but all of them were shot down or taken prisoner. The English army now advanced in line to take possession of the field of battle, mopping up as they did so any small pockets of resistance that remained.

The plunderers in the rear seem to have melted away, and by about three o'clock in the afternoon the only Frenchmen to be seen on the field were the prisoners and the innumerable dead and wounded.

As soon as the last of the enemy had been captured or chased away, the King called for silence and thanked his men for so bravely risking their lives in his service. He warned them, however, not to be so blinded by pride as to attribute their astonishing victory either to his leadership or to their own prowess, but to recognise that a miracle had been granted by God to humble the pride of the French. He added rather priggishly that the defeat of the enemy proved that his claims in France were just and righteous. Though he later admitted that the defeat of the French had been partly due to their indisciplines and bad tactics, Henry, like most of his men, really believed in the miraculous nature of the victory, and for the rest of his life he refused to accept any direct praise for his own part in it.

For almost four hours after the end of the battle the English remained in the field, hardly able to believe that the French would not return and attack them again. During this time the archers wandered amongst the heaps of bodies, looking for anyone still alive and worth ransoming, and stripping and pillaging the dead. Valuable armour was piled onto horses and carried back to the English quarters in Maisoncelles, and so great was the plunder that the King had to order that each man should only take away what he could easily carry on the march.

Meanwhile the King and his nobles walked about the battlefield, and Henry sent for the heralds of both sides, who had taken no part in the battle but had stood together as spectators. He formally asked the senior French herald, Mountjoy, to whom the victory belonged, and received the answer that it belonged to the English. He then asked the name of the nearest fortress to the field — after which, by the law of arms, the battle should be called — and was told that it was Agincourt. After this curiously ritualistic ceremony the heralds returned to their melancholy task of counting and recording the dead.

At about seven o'clock in the evening, as the darkness and the rain came on together, the English left the field and retired to Maisoncelles, where most of them fell into an exhausted sleep. The King, it is said, dined in state, waited on by the noblest of his captives. The bodies of the English dead — save for those of the Duke of York and the Earl of Suffolf, which were boiled so that their bones could be taken to England — were piled together in a barn and burnt, the flames continuing all night.

Meanwhile, those French wounded that could limp or crawl got themselves into the woods or the neighbouring villages, where many of them were murdered by the peasants for their clothes or armour. The dead, and those too badly hurt to move, were stripped naked during the night either by the French villagers or the English soldiery. Any who were unfortunate enough to survive the night were clubbed to death in the morning by the English army as it passed, loaded with plunder, on its triumphant way to Calais.

5: Conclusions

IT IS difficult for us to grasp the magnitude of the English victory; many of those who were present looked upon it more as an act of God than a battle, and some of them even claimed to have seen a vision of St. George in the sky above the English army. Certainly, for generations, and even centuries, afterwards the French looked upon their defeat as a punishment from God for the sins of their nation. Even in this cynical age, there still seems to be something of the miraculous in the fact that 6,000 sick and weary men could not only beat off, but utterly rout, an army perhaps ten times as large.

"Never since Christ was born" said a Parisian chronicler when he heard the news of the battle, "has anyone done so much damage to France." Between seven and ten thousand Frenchmen were killed, most of them the members of the nobility and gentry who had charged in the vanguard and the main-body. Amongst the dead were the Constable Charles d'Albret, the Dukes of Brabant, Alençon and Bar, the Admiral of France, the Archbishop of Sens, seven counts, over 220 lords and barons and four or five thousand knights and esquires. A whole generation of the French nobility, in fact, was wiped off the face of the earth, and a local chronicler recorded that, of all the knights whose lands lay around Agincourt, only one was left alive. Two thousand more Frenchmen including the Dukes of Orleans and Bourbon, Jean de Boucicault, Marshal of France, three counts and fourteen barons, were carried off as prisoners to England, whence many of them never returned.

Perhaps worse for France than the slaughter of her nobility, however, was the national disgrace of a defeat where tens of thousands of Frenchmen had fled without striking a blow. The shame of Agincourt hung over French soldiers for a generation, during which they lost battle after battle to the English, and was only dispelled by the almost supernatural intervention of Joan of Arc, the Holy Maid of France.

On the English side — again almost miraculously — the losses were remarkably small, though it is hard to believe the chroniclers who assure us that only 25 or so men were killed in all. Casualties of five or six hundred are more likely, the majority of them being archers or men-at-arms from the right-wing which had taken the first brunt of the French charge. Of the noblemen only the Duke of York and the Earl of Suffolk were killed, for the Duke of Gloucester soon recovered from his wound. Five or six knights are known to have fallen, including Sir Richard Kyghley from Lancashire, and, from Breconshire, Sir Daffydd ap Llewlleyn Fychan, better known as Fluellen or as Davy Gam. It is likely that the last — an old comrade of the King's famous for his attempt to murder Owen Glendower — was in the royal bodyguard, with his two sons-in-law Sir Walter Lloyd and Roger Vaughan, both of whom were killed.

What brought about the complete rout of the French by the much smaller English force? We have already seen that the French army was undisciplined, divided, and without a real leader. It was teetering on the brink of anarchy before the battle began, and at the first setback it collapsed into total chaos. Lesser factors operating against the French were the mud, which seems to have affected them more than it did the English, and the woods on each side of the field, which cramped their huge formations.

The English, though in worse physical condition than the French, were a united and disciplined army of determined men, under one powerful leader, whose ability to inspire men was phenomenal. They had the advantage of the ground, for the woods that hemmed in the French served to protect the flanks of their defensive position.

Witnesses on both sides agree that the main deciding factors of the battle were the English archers, who destroyed the French cavalry charge, forced the enemy men-at-arms into a position where they were so cramped as to be helpless, and then attacked them hand to hand. In praising the archers, however, we should not forget the steadfastness of the English men-at-arms, who bore the first brunt of the French dismounted attack, stopped it in its tracks, and then held it off for two or three hours of ceaseless fighting.

Though it is unfashionable to say so, it is also at least partly true that the English won the battle because most of them were brave men, and that the French lost it because many of them were cowards.

THE END

Appendix: An English Muster Roll

THE FOLLOWING is a full and direct translation of the muster roll of the company under the command of Sir Richard de Kyghley, who came from Inskip in Lancashire, and who was killed in the battle. The original, which is in old French, is kept with several other Agincourt muster rolls amongst the manuscripts of the Public Record Office, London. The spelling of the soldiers' names has been left in its original form.

The first section (Public Record Office reference E101/46/3) is a list of Sir Richard's own retinue, including several members of his own family amongst the men at arms. The second part (E/101/4429) gives the names of the fifty Lancashire archers raised by the sheriff of Lancashire and placed under Sir Richard's command.

As we can see from this list, Sir Richard's company were rather unfortunate. Of a total of 74 men, no less than 31 were put out of action during the course of the campaign. Five, including Sir Richard himself, were killed in the battle, seven died of disease, twelve were invalided home, and seven taken prisoner. These high losses were probably not typical of the English army as a whole: in a retinue of comparable size, that of Sir Thomas Erpingham (E101/47/20), only seven men were lost of a total of eighty. Of these, four were invalided home, two died of disease, one died between Harfleur and Agincourt, and only one was killed in the battle.

These are the names of the men-at-arms who were retained with Richard de Kyghley:

Sir Richard de Kyghley
he was killed at the battle of Agincourt
Thomas de Kyghley
he died at Harfleur three days after the town was taken
Robert de Kyghley
William de Walton
they were at the battle of Agincourt and went to Calais and then to England with five horses
William de Pemberton
Thurstannolde Standyssh
they were sick and had license from the King to go to England after the town was taken

The archers of the same Sir Richard:

killed at the battle of Agincourt

William de Holland	Robert de Bradshawe
John Grenebogh	Gilbert Howson

these were at the said battle and went to Calais and from Calais to London with twelve of their own horses and six horses of the said Sir Richard

Hugh del Bonk	Henry Frenche
John del Wood	Hugh del Twisse
Richard Beme	William Osbarne
John Hunt	John Harper
Adam del Brigge	Thomas Shawlyn
John del Brigge	John Bredkuke
John Alanson	Nicholas Blakeborne

These are the names of the fifty archers who were put under the command of the late Sir Richard de Kyghley in the realm of France, by order of the King in the third year of his reign:

these were at the battle of Agincourt and went to Calais and from Calais to London with eight horses

Thomas le Wyght
Thomas Aynesworth
John Archebald
Seth de Tildesley
Thomas de Pecford
John de Tildesley
Edward le Baxter
John de Halghton
John Tomson
Dicon Robinson
Richard de Bolton
John del Shagh
Henry Hamson
Thomas Hamson
Henry Wynard
Henry de Tildesley
Richard Archibold
Thomas de Leylond
Thomas de Lyndeley

these were taken prisoner the day before the battle
(Author's note: Details of how they were captured are unknown)

William le Flode
Thomas Archibold
Thomas Hesketh
Robert le Sclater
Thomas le Taillour
William le Taillour
William Lynche

these died during the siege of Harfleur

William de Thornton
William Taillour of Ormskirk
Nicholas de Kilay

William Taillour of Inskip
William Pynchebek
Hugo del Lawe

these were left at Harfleur for the defence of the same

Thomas Styrop
Henry Culcheth
Matthew Gardener
Thomas Dounhede
John Dynyng
Richard Dynyng
Thomas Bynison
John Deke

these were sick and had license from the King to go to England after Harfleur was taken

John Dicinson
Edward le Glover
William de Scaldon
William Sharp
Richard de Shapley
Thomas le Milner
Richard Thomas
Richard le Parker
William le Barbur
William de Sandall
